GRAPHIC HISTORY

THE ASSASSINATION OF ABRAHAM
LINCOLN

by Kay Melchisedech Olson

illustrated by
Otha Zackariah Edward Lohse

Consultant:
Thomas F. Schwartz, PhD
Illinois State Historian
Illinois Historic Preservation Agency
Springfield, Illinois

Capstone
press

Mankato, Minnesota

Graphic Library is published by Capstone Press,
1710 Roe Crest Drive, North Mankato, Minnesota 56003.
www.capstonepub.com

Library of Congress Cataloging-in-Publication Data
Olson, Kay Melchisedech.
The assassination of Abraham Lincoln / by Kay Melchisedech Olson; illustrated by Otha
Zackariah Edward Lohse.
    p. cm.—(Graphic library. Graphic history)
Includes bibliographical references (p.31) and index.
Audience: Grades 4–6.
ISBN: 978-0-7368-3831-3 (hardcover)
ISBN: 978-0-7368-5241-8 (paperback)
    1. Lincoln, Abraham, 1809–1865—Assassination—Juvenile literature. 2. Booth, John
Wilkes, 1838–1865—Juvenile literature. I. Lohse, Otha Zackariah Edward. II. Title. III. Series.
E457.5.O48 2005
973.7'092—dc22   2004020300

Summary: In graphic-novel format, tells the story of Abraham Lincoln's assassination and the
escape and death of John Wilkes Booth.

Editor's note: Direct quotations from primary sources are indicated by a yellow background.

Direct quotations appear on the following pages:
Page 5 (Lincoln), from *Twenty Days* by Dorothy Meserve Kunhardt and Philip B. Kunhardt Jr.
(New York: Castle Books, 1965).
Pages 5 (actor), 8, 19, 21, 27, from *Blood on the Moon* by Edward Steers (Lexington: University
Press of Kentucky, 2001).
Pages 13, 20, from *The Day Lincoln Was Shot* by Jim Bishop (New York: Harper & Row, 1955).

Credits
Art Director and Storyboard Artist
Jason Knudson

Art Director
Heather Kindseth

Editor
Tom Adamson

Acknowledgement
Capstone Press thanks Philip Charles
Crawford, Library Director, Essex High
School, Essex, Vermont, and columnist
for *Knowledge Quest*, for his assistance
in the preparation of this book.

Table of Contents

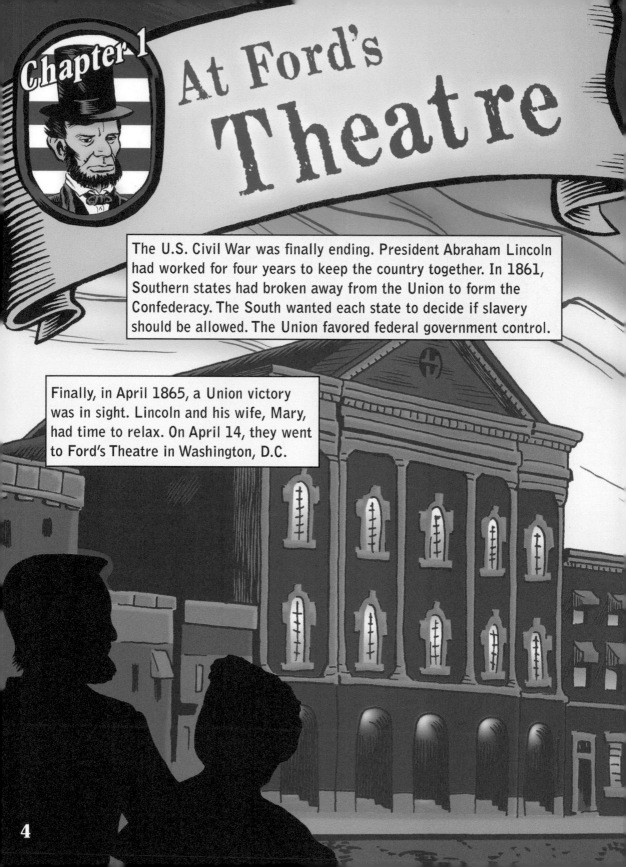

Chapter 1

At Ford's Theatre

The U.S. Civil War was finally ending. President Abraham Lincoln had worked for four years to keep the country together. In 1861, Southern states had broken away from the Union to form the Confederacy. The South wanted each state to decide if slavery should be allowed. The Union favored federal government control.

Finally, in April 1865, a Union victory was in sight. Lincoln and his wife, Mary, had time to relax. On April 14, they went to Ford's Theatre in Washington, D.C.

Just then, a man slowly walked up the stairs to the state box. John Wilkes Booth was an actor but was not part of the show.

Booth carried a gun and a dagger. He had backed the South during the Civil War. A month earlier, Booth had plotted with others to kidnap Lincoln.

Tonight, Booth had other plans.

As he landed, Booth broke a bone in his left leg above the ankle. But he still managed to escape.

The group went to William Petersen's boardinghouse across the street.

We need your best room for President Lincoln.

The men put Lincoln diagonally on the bed because it was too short for his tall frame.

Robert, Lincoln's oldest son, had been at the White House when his father was shot. Upon hearing the news, Robert immediately went to Petersen's boardinghouse. He tried to calm his mother throughout the night.

Here is a chair, Mother. Please sit down.

Oh, I wish my little Taddy could see his father before he dies!

Secretary of War Edwin Stanton stepped in to restore order to the room.

Take that woman out and do not let her in again.

Oh . . . I have given my husband to die!

The doctors in the room gathered around Lincoln's bed. Their only treatment was to remove blood clots that formed over the bullet wound. Lincoln's breathing began to slow.

At 7:22 in the morning, President Lincoln died.

Now he belongs to the ages.

The doctor placed coins on Lincoln's eyes to keep them closed, as was the custom at the time.

Chapter 4
The End of Booth

What happened?

With a broken bone tearing the flesh of his leg, John Wilkes Booth escaped from Washington, D.C. He rode to the Surratt Tavern in Maryland. There, he met his friend David Herold. Herold had helped Booth with his plot to kill Lincoln.

Continuing south from the tavern, Booth and Herold arrived at the home of Dr. Samuel Mudd. Word of what happened to President Lincoln had not yet reached Mudd's home.

After treating Booth's leg, Dr. Mudd offered the two men food and let them rest.

That afternoon, Booth and Herold headed out on horseback. They stopped at the home of a Southern sympathizer, Colonel Samuel Cox.

Here is enough food to last four days. Good luck to you!

Booth and Herold traveled south for several days. On April 24, they made it to a ferry at Port Conway, in King George County, Virginia.

Here's a true hero, boys! He shot and killed the Union president!

They then made their way to the Virginia farm of Richard Garrett to hide out.

Booth refused to surrender.

Well, my brave boys, you can prepare a stretcher for me. I will never surrender.

Soldiers set the barn on fire. They could see Booth through the cracks and knotholes in the burning barn. He had a rifle.

Without orders, soldier Boston Corbett fired his pistol into the barn. Booth was hit and fell.

Quick, help pull him out while there's still time.

Booth was shot through the neck. Soldiers carried him to the porch of the Garrett house. There, Booth lived about three hours. Around 7:00 in the morning, he uttered his final words.

Tell my mother I die for my country.

- The Civil War began on April 12, 1861. Confederate General Lee surrendered to Union General Grant on April 9, 1865, at Appomattox Court House in Virginia. Five days later, Lincoln was assassinated.

- In March 1865, John Wilkes Booth visited Charles Warwick, a friend and fellow actor. Warwick was living in a room at the Petersen boardinghouse. During his visit, Warwick let Booth take a nap on the bed. One month later, President Lincoln died on the same bed.

- Booth's deed was part of a conspiracy. Confederate sympathizers wanted to create chaos in the federal government. They planned to kill the president, vice president, secretary of state, and Union General Grant. Lincoln was the only one to actually die.

- The U.S. government charged eight people with the conspiracy. Four people were sentenced to be hanged, three to life in prison, and one to a six-year prison term.

- Abraham Lincoln was born February 12, 1809. When he died on April 15, 1865, he was 56 years old.

- Lincoln was inaugurated as the 16th president on March 4, 1861. He was reelected to a second term, which began on March 4, 1865.

- Lincoln was the first president to be photographed at his inauguration. John Wilkes Booth can be seen standing close to Lincoln in the picture.

- Lincoln was the first president to have a beard while in offIce.

- At 6 feet, 4 inches tall, Lincoln was the tallest president.

- Vice President Andrew Johnson became president on April 15, 1865, hours after Lincoln died.

- Each fall and spring, the Surratt Society sponsors bus tours along Booth's escape route. People can also follow Booth's path by car. Today, the route has paved roads and is lined with businesses. In 1865, it was a muddy, swampy path.

Glossary

assassin (uh-SASS-uhn)—a person who murders a well-known or important person, such as a president

chaos (KAY-oss)—total confusion

conspiracy (kuhn-SPIHR-uh-see)—a secret, illegal plan made by two or more people

ferry (FER-ee)—a boat or ship that regularly carries people across a stretch of water

mortal (MOR-tuhl)—causing death; Lincoln's gunshot wound was mortal.

plot (PLOT)—to plan in secret, usually to do something wrong or illegal

sympathizer (SIM-puh-thyz-uhr)—a person who supports a group or a cause

tyrant (TYE-ruhnt)—someone who rules other people in a cruel or unjust way

Internet Sites

FactHound offers a safe, fun way to find Internet sites related to this book. All of the sites on FactHound have been researched by our staff.

Here's how:

1. Visit *www.facthound.com*
2. Type in this special code **0736838317** for age-appropriate sites. Or enter a search word related to this book for a more general search.
3. Click on the **Fetch It** button.

FactHound will fetch the best sites for you!

Read More

Burgan, Michael. *The Assassination of Abraham Lincoln*. We the People. Minneapolis: Compass Point Books, 2004.

Marinelli, Deborah A. *The Assassination of Abraham Lincoln*. The Library of Political Assassinations. New York: Rosen, 2002.

Oberle, Lora Polack. *Abraham Lincoln*. Let Freedom Ring. Mankato, Minn.: Bridgestone Books, 2002.

Schott, Jane A. *Abraham Lincoln*. History Maker Bios. Minneapolis: Lerner, 2002.

Zeinert, Karen. *The Lincoln Murder Plot*. North Haven, Conn.: Linnet Books, 1999.

Bibliography

Bishop, Jim. *The Day Lincoln Was Shot*. New York: Harper & Row, 1955.

Bryan, George S. *The Great American Myth*. Chicago: Americana House, 1990.

Ford's Theatre National Historic Site. http://www.nps.gov/foth/index2.htm.

Kunhardt, Dorothy Meserve, and Philip B. Kunhardt Jr. *Twenty Days*. New York: Castle Books, 1965.

Norton, Roger. Abraham Lincoln Research Site. http://members.aol.com/RVSNorton/Lincoln2.html.

Steers, Edward Jr. *Blood on the Moon: The Assassination of Abraham Lincoln*. Lexington: University Press of Kentucky, 2001.

Index